APPLE HARVEST

BEATA DUNCAN

*Gwen Hartland
With best wishes
Beata Duncan*

HEARING EYE

HEARING EYE
Torriano Meeting House Poetry Pamphlet No. 28
ISBN 1 870841 72 7
© Beata Duncan 2000

Typeset by Daniel James at mondo designo
Cover drawing by Marilyn Rogers

Some of these poems first appeared in New Poetry Vols. 4, 6 & 7 (Arts Council & Hutchinson), London Magazine, New Statesman, The Observer, The Rialto, The Spectator, Women's Review and The Express.

A Man Who Knew What He Wanted and *Christmas Card* were awarded prizes in the National Poetry Competition. *Keeping Time* and *Apple Harvest* have recently been set to music by Richard Arnell.

This publication has been made possible with the financial assistance of the London Arts Board.

CONTENTS

Keeping Time	4
Mothers and Fathers	5
A Kinder Egg	6
Apple Harvest	7
The Cottage in Zennor and a Slice of Grapefruit	8
Presents	10
A Commonplace Day	11
Agony Aunt	12
Encounter	12
Christmas Card	13
Free Facial	14
Magritte's Colonial Friend	15
Seasonal Compliment	16
Aristocrat in the Air	17
A Man Who Knew What He Wanted	18
Poor Jack	19
Untied States	20
Blood of Strangers	21
The Lovely Butcheress	22
Anne Frank's Pin-Ups	24
Saying Good-bye	26

KEEPING TIME

For days I couldn't find
the watch you gave me,
small certainty on my left wrist.
I looked in the usual places,
fingered the empty box
and read the guarantee for consolation.

Searching, I came upon
a pocket watch of solid gold,
a hand-down from an ancestor,
kept in a cotton sock.
An eighth or a sixteenth of me,
he wore it ticking near his heart.

The winding button turned
and made a grating noise,
the ornate arrows didn't budge.
I slipped it back into
the darkness of the drawer,
where it will say forever four to six.

'You've got your watch' you ask
when I steal a glance at yours.
'Of course!' I am resolved
to buy a replica,
'just giving it a rest.'

Changing the sheets,
I find it lying in a fold
face upwards, shining,
strap curved to the shape of my wrist.

MOTHERS AND FATHERS

Andy was jubilant about the baby.
'I'm going to have a brother!'
he told his friends
and put some soldiers
in a Smartie box.

Mum did her best to make him accept
that it could be a girl;
she grew bigger and rounder.
Andy hugged the warm globe

and heard the heartbeat,
felt the kicks.
Soon his sister would come
and they'd play mothers and fathers.

Dad pointed out that it might,
after all, be a boy.
Andy was unperturbed:
'That's alright' he said,
'we'll dress him up in a skirt.'

A KINDER EGG
For Robert and Ifor Raphael

We waited in the kitchen,
the midwife thought
it wouldn't be long.
The house was quiet
except for quick steps
to the bathroom and back.

I began to read
'The owl and the pussycat
went to sea...' but Andy
had his eyes on the door —
he'd waited for the baby
for a hundred years!

I said 'I'll buy you
a little present',
he chose a Kinder Egg.
Black and orange bits
fell from the chocolate shell

onto the kitchen table;
munching, he assembled
a dark warrior
with bright headdress
and a loincloth.

The smiling midwife left;
a reddish wrinkled face
nestled in the bedclothes.
Andy laid down his chieftain,
the first gift to his brother.

APPLE HARVEST

It was all just right:
snow in December,
no frost in spring
to hurt the blossom
and a hot hot June.

Our trees stood close,
heavy with ripening fruit;
the end one leaned towards the cottage,
branches touching the ground.
At night the apples stood out pale
like solid moons.

We took the pippins first
and left them under the weeping willow
for coolness;
The drawer of gran's old wardrobe
was heaped with fruit.

The parent tree moved in the wind,
yellow leaves among the green

an emptiness about its freedom.

THE COTTAGE IN ZENNOR AND A SLICE OF GRAPEFRUIT

For a whole week I had a house
where Lawrence lived some sixty years before.
Two smallish rooms, one up one down
near Land's End
where the Atlantic rushes in.

One day I cut a grapefruit into three,
making a cartwheel of the middle,
removed a segment
and peered through the hole.
In the blue distance I could see
the raised arm of the Statue of Liberty.

Passing the house, someone would say:
'he had it for five pounds a year'
in cultured unCornish tones,
'his landlord was a Captain Short.'

Or they would knock
while I was still at breakfast
to ask me about D.H.L.
'I don't know who you mean!'
'You've heard' they'd say 'of Lady Chat?'
'Oh yes, I've heard about all that.
You'd better go to Nottingham... and Robin Hood.
Or Croydon, where he slept all night
and taught young boys from nine to four.'

I shut the door
and put my finger on the mantelpiece
where he had carved his letters: D.H.L.
Up on the wall
his phoenix rose from zigzag flames
but now was whitewashed over.

When I looked out again
the sinking sun flashed blue
and vanished,
as it does off Zennor.
I sprinkled sugar
on the grapefruit wheel,
restored the missing piece
and ate the whole with relish,
as he would have wished.

PRESENTS

Before Fred went to Spain
I gave him spinach from the market,
full of iron and vitamins.
He gave me fresh mackerel

which I put in my fridge
beside a tub of cottage cheese;
day after day I meant to cook it,
the fridge began to stink.

I took the mackerel out —
cold and beautiful, pink flesh,
grey skin with rib-like markings
on the back — and buried it

by the rhododendron bush
to rot and feed the roots.
When the mauve blooms opened,
I'd remember.

Fred got back and rang me:
'Come round for a paella.'
I took a bottle of wine.
He was tanned

and said he felt wonderful.
My bouquet of spinach leaves
lay on his draining board,
wilted and dry.

A COMMONPLACE DAY

My floor cloth has a hole in it,
I wring out the dirty water;
the kitchen floor is clean.

My husband is eating his egg,
he does not love me.
My son is eating his egg,
it is all over his chin.
He has one tooth and he loves me.

My friend has sent a card
from Cornwall. At Land's End
waves mount and spit and crash,
it is frightening.

My son sits in his bath
and blows ripples
to the edge of the tub.
He has got ten toes, so have I;
we are lucky.

My daughter comes home from school
and puts on her brownie uniform.
When she smiles
she looks like her father;
she gives me a kiss and is gone.

'Your bus fare!' I call after her.
She turns and smiles
and waves and goes running,
running into the dusk.
Her tunic is a brown balloon.

My husband loved me once,
he will buy me a new floor cloth.

AGONY AUNT

He says you have nothing in common,
keeps to his side of the bed,
never wears his knitted slippers.

A white mouse hanging from a pierced ear
by a silver thread
can be wonderfully diverting.

But take the rodent off at bedtime
and hang a picture of your neck
in the mouse house, to make it feel secure.

You may write to me whenever you like.

ENCOUNTER

Cypresses lean towards each other
like women gossiping,
then straighten,
shaking a little at the tips.
'I have not said
what I have said.'

The wind blows up again —
they dance and pitch
in wild confusion,
flaunting light and sombre green.
'What I have said
I have not said!'

Centrally heated,
double glazed,
I cower in my quilted dressing gown.
'What I have thought
I have not thought.'

CHRISTMAS CARD

The first one to arrive is from
a childhood friend in Illinois,
a large card sent by air
with 'Water Lilies' by Monet.
Her news is scrawled inside:

Cars for the twins at Christmas,
the garage is too small!
Sheets of ice float on
Lake Michigan... right now
she chairs a Committee

for Human Relations.
There is so much green
reflected in the water;
the shadowy figure of a child
with long hair and a hat

is looking in the lush confusion
for something lost. Is this card one
of two hundred for the family list —
business connections,
couples met on holiday?

I look on the back:
painted a year before his death,
it is an old man's masterpiece.
Yet he left out the bridge
across his water garden.

FREE FACIAL

A trial offer from
the Health and Beauty Clinic
in the High Street.
The beautician wears white sandals
and a starched white overall.

The esoteric ritual begins
with gritty cleansing —
apricot kernels, she explains,
her lined and treated face
suspended over mine.

Blue liquid in a bottle
looks like diluted ink;
it's full of living cells,
she won't wipe any of it off.

Yes, they are placental cells
from a black Australian sheep
raised near Lake Geneva.
Yes, the mother sheep is killed
but it is done humanely.

Now the mask: swabs on eyelids,
a cooling mudlike substance
spreads and stiffens on my face.
She leaves me sightless
and goes to fetch free samples;

comes back with minute silver boxes
and the price list,
which is staggering. Shall we
make the next appointment?

For days my face feels
soft and firm. I touch it
with the back of my hand
and think of starched white linen,

blue water in a bottle
and Lake Geneva,
where an expectant mother
was humanely killed.

MAGRITTE'S COLONIAL FRIEND

took his foot out of a snowball
and examined it for lice —
Such elegant toe nails!

Then he said to his
Malayan mango boy
'Gentleman, you may smoke!'

SEASONAL COMPLIMENT

The sycamore outside my window
turned deep red again, as if to say:
'I renew my beauty every year
and you are now completely grey.'

Rain fell and put a shine
on its leaves,
I had my hair tinted
and bought a new dress.

He came at teatime
with his bunch of chrysanthemums,
hair carefully combed
over balding patch,

and saw me standing there
in the window.
'Your tree looks wonderful!'
he said with that charm of his.

ARISTOCRAT IN THE AIR

His head moves up and down in sleep,
hands in pale silk cuffs
closed on the *Times*.

He left mixed vegetables
on his plastic plate,
I wrap a tiny loaf in a large napkin
for my hosts.

'Blinds down for the movie!'
Hidden lamps spread a garish half-light,
grey flex grows from his ears,
eyes fix the screen.

I dream about a snowman
who puts a carrot in his face,
I yoyo with his cuff-links;

his name is Yoyo Marx
from Ellis island. Once he proposed
to the Statue of Liberty;
a chilly tear drops in my ear.

The cast list slides up the screen,
My neighbour opens his *Times*.
I search the sky for Yoyo Marx —

it turns into white waves,
ears pop,
we sink under flying clouds
to straight lines of Manhattan.

A MAN WHO KNEW WHAT HE WANTED

When he was young he bought a bra
for a girl with a good figure,
if he should meet one;
white with buttons
and a little flower.

The years went by
and he found no girl to suit;
he met some nice ones, to be sure,
but they were always
too large or too small.

Sometimes he washed the bra
and filled it with mothballs;
once he put his hands round,
to feel.

When he became a pensioner
he tidied up his house,
made it nice and snug;
lit a fire with logs and branches
from the woods
and warmed his empty hands.

He took the brassière
from the chest beside his bed
and sewed a new flower on it,
just in case.

POOR JACK

Jack suddenly became a widower.
He was watching 'Golden Girls'
at the time,
his wife was pinning
a rip in the bedspread.

The women in the block
expected her to grow old with them;
she was only sixty-eight,
poor Rosie...
there were tears in their eyes.

Jack said he'd had enough happiness
to last a lifetime,
but they rallied round.
Sandra threw away the wallflowers,
Millicent defrosted the fridge,

Betty baked a cake. Grace offered
to sew the torn counterpane,
but Prunella said: 'Let me!
I can patch candlewick
so it won't even show!'

UNTIED STATES

'Dear little girl!' the old Queen called you
outside a jeweller's shop in Windsor.
Now, beside your granny chair,
I remind you of the story. You smile,
a soft grey down about your mouth.
'Oh, did she?'

Books line the wall beneath the dado;
above it Japanese prints,
your water colour of the Suffolk cottage.
Trees outside hide other houses.

His books, with which you helped,
are in a case, his entry in the D.N.B.
'He told me once you typed Untied
for United States.'
'Oh, did I... why did he die?'

I glimpse his sculpted head
in the Venetian mirror
and stroke the white hood of your hair
with the thin plait.
'Shall we read a page of Henry James?'

You fix me with blue eyes:
'There's nothing that I have that I want...
no, that can't be right, can it?'
I gesture round the room:
'All this is yours, it is your home!'
'Oh, is it!'

The carer brings your pills,
plumps up a cushion; she is tanned,
specks of gold glisten on her arms.
'Having a nice chat?' She cups your chin.
'Give us a smile, sweetheart!'
And you do.

BLOOD OF STRANGERS

High up on a metal stand
blood drips into
a narrow plastic heart
and down a long thin tube
plugged into Lucy's arm.
She sits here hour after hour,

the blood of strangers
fills her veins.
But Lucy is unchanged:
quick-tempered, witty, kind,
her reddish curls are back
and roses bloom

on black silk pants.
We chat about Tim's school report
and garden furniture;
soon we will sit in deckchairs
by the lily pond
and watch the frog.

Outside the hospital
I buy a rosebud
wrapped in cellophane.
The man hands it across his stall,
blond hairs sunlit on tanned arm.

THE LOVELY BUTCHERESS

Dear Cath, I am sitting by the fire
with my coat on,
drinking tea out of your mug;
just back from the Arts Centre and
'The Spirit of Berlin in the Twenties'.
You said Richard Ziegler
would be worth a visit.

He painted a lot of women
with high cheekbones and big velvet eyes;
housewives with low hats and fur collars
(like that photo of gran
teaching mum to ride a bike),
prostitutes in scanty clothes.

The one that really got to me
is called 'Die Schoene Metzgerin' —
The lovely butcheress:
a pantry with the carcass of a boar
and a stout young woman,
naked except for stockings and shoes,
belly touching the pig's.

Her features are very fine:
straight nose, full lips, long lashes.
She is raising the penis from dead entrails
and touching it with the tip of a knife,
a look of utter contentment on her face —
or 'satisfaction' would be the better word.

The colours are mostly warm:
pink for the two bodies,
rich brown stockings and cottage loaf hair;
dabs of red for her mouth
and the pig's clotted blood.

But her heels are black and square
on chequered floor tiles,
the grey hooks through his trotters
tone in with her gleaming knife.

What is he saying in that painting?
I went back again and again —
what, for God's sake,
does that say about me?

The gallery was almost empty,
only an old man looking at the women,
and I didn't meet anyone
on my way home.

I bought a catalogue for you —
Please come back soon!

'The Spirit of Berlin in the Twenties' was an exhibition of Richard Ziegler's work at the Camden Arts Centre. The painting 'Die Schoene Metzgerin' is at the V&A.

ANNE FRANK'S PIN-UPS

Your room is bare of furniture
but otherwise the same
as on the day you went:
green window frames and yellow beams,
faded paper with brown leaves and twigs.

And your pin-ups, sticky tape
still on them under glass.
The largest is a watermill
with poplars and a bridge,
and an advertisement for jam.

In a group apart Princess Juliana
with a baby on her lap (exiled in England
while you were hiding in the Prinsengracht),
'Elizabeth and Margaret Rose of York',
the elder sister seated,
the little one in ankle socks.

(Where your parents slept,
the children's growth is marked
by pencil lines.)

Greta Garbo with long lashes
and an eyebrow painted
like a thin dark leaf,
giving her face the nature of a mime.

Ginger Rogers, Ray Milland —
the stars were 'all mixed up together'
you wrote in your diary,
'simply gasping to be tidied up'.

A German postcard of a dimpled child,
plucking petals from a daisy:
'Er liebt mich... he loves me
a little, with all his heart,
beyond all measure,
can't leave off.'

The only object standing in the room
is your bronze head on a black pedestal;
it casts a shadow on your pin-up
of a star.

SAYING GOOD-BYE
For Duncan Burn

I had not seen your eyes closed,
only when your lids fluttered
to make a point.

On the altar the cross
in which you did not believe
and your daughter's narcissi.

They have dressed you in white
with a lace-trimmed collar.
'Prophet out of his time'
a critic wrote.

Your book is on my shelf,
only half read.
I didn't ask for explanations
or say I broke
the grey-striped vase you gave me;
the pieces felt so thin.

Brushed back, your hair
shows traces of colour
I had forgotten;
face smooth, folds gone,
mouth slightly open as in sleep.

I want to stand you up
like a doll from its crib
so you can give me coffee
after dinner,

help me into my coat
and leave the front door open
until I close the garden gate
and wave.

Saying good-bye
my voice breaks on your name,
engraved in steel on the coffin lid
standing by the door.

For a complete list of Hearing Eye publications, please write enclosing an SAE to: Hearing Eye, Box 1, 99 Torriano Avenue, London NW5 2RX

Alternatively, please visit the Hearing Eye website at: http://www.torriano.org